If I

What would you (
If I told you a
All my lies   …, pain

What would you do if I told you how I felt?
How you made me see the differences in the world and its people
The changes in me that people said would never happen.
What would you do if I told you I had aids?
A virus so deadly so many people won't come near me
They fear that if they do they will catch it and die.
What would you do if I told you I explained they couldn't inherit the disease from a touch?
If I told you that in spite of all my explanations to them they still fear me or at least the disease;
How can I live when no one wants to be around?
When I am alone…
What if I told you that I had imaginings about committing suicide?
How would you help me or would you try to hurt me?
If I told you about my family and all they have done to me
How would that make you feel?
Would you care? Or would you be like the others and leave?
I am afraid to be alone with only doctors to comfort me;
Strangers, people who I do not know.
If I told you all the worries I have had
All the people who are like me, that share my feelings of neglect and pain
If I told you about the voices I have heard telling me to let go and give in
If I told you about my pursuit to live
If I told you all of this would you even care?
Would you stay?
Love me?
Hold me?
Fight with me to live?
If I told you all these things what would be your response?
Would you dare me to keep fighting?
Knowing in your heart I have a chance to live if I don't give in
To the voice that keeps calling me all through the day
"Give in, Let go, come to me… Give in!" It says to me
Would you let me know that I would live to be a hundred if I told you?
If I told you I had aids?
Or would you quote the statistics and tell me how I would die?

Pressure me into letting go and giving in?
How can I trust you if I don't know these things?
Can you tell me this?
If I told you the truth about me
Share with you my deepest secret and darkest fear
Tell me, what you would do
If I Told You

Truth Be Told

If you knew the truth about me would you come around? Would you look at me the way you do that makes my heart flutter? Would you look at me the same way when you told me you loved me? How would our relationship have changed if you knew I could die from this disease? Truth Be Told, you don't have a clue, do you? If the truth were laid upon you again and again you wouldn't know how to deal with it. How can I deal with it if you can't see past your own doubts and frustrations? You are the person I look to- to see a future- if I fight this disease. Truth, I don't know, all I would know is that if I didn't deal with this I would die quicker. Truth Be Told, I am scared of this disease. I know what it can do to me and what it could do to us. I know how it can tare a family apart and make a person feel like the world has forgotten them. That is how I feel at this very moment. I've been and am going through these stages. I don't know who my friends are because this disease has pushed so many people away from me. I live with this on a day-to-day basis and the only end in sight that I see is death. But I am not ready to die. I don't feel that it is my time. I know there is no cure for this, only speculation as to how we can survive longer with it. Truth Be Told, those doctors out there don't even know if their plan will work; they can only hope. Truth Be Told, I am a fool for you. I believe that you will stay with me even after you have found out the truth of me. The dark secret people told you I had and didn't tell you about. But it's over now, no more lies: I told you what I had hidden from you. I told you the dark secret I kept hidden from you. Kept hidden, because I did not want you to hate me once you discovered my true identity. Truth Be Told, I thought you would have found out a long time ago, so that I could have explained things to you. So I could have explained all those times during intercourse I made you use protection. Why, when you tried to go down, I would say, "No! Stay up and hold me instead." The reasons why I would make sure I was clean on a daily basis. Haven't you wondered why I took those pills? Why the reasons I was taking them seemed to change over time. Have you ever wondered why I never let you in? Or get close to me because I thought you could see through me and see the disease. Truth Be Told, you probably knew from the beginning and didn't say anything. You probably didn't know what to say; How to react once you heard the news about the disease that infected my body. You probably figured I would tell you and decided to play it safe by not saying anything. Truth Be Told, how can I blame you for acting the way you have? Not being around when I needed you and being distant over the years that we've spent together. I cannot blame you for any of that. I can only ask, "If I did not have this disease would that be enough for you to stay?" Or is this disease the answer you needed to leave me? Truth Be Told, you probably won't tell me. I will be sleep one night and awake the next morning to find you gone. A note by my pillow written by you telling me how sorry you are and how you would pray for me. Telling me how you had to move out of fear. Would I cry? Yes. But in the end I would know the truth. I am alone in this battle. If I don't fight for me no one else will and it will just be me in the end. Those who said they care only stay for a brief time and then leave me to fin for myself. I can't tell you how many times I wake up feeling along and scared. How I would cry at night because you were not here with me. Truth Be Told, if your expression is anything to go by, you probably don't care about me. You probably don't care about all the things I am saying to you at this very moment. You are probably thinking about the best way to escape. Why? Why would you leave me vulnerable like this after all that we have been through together? I can't tell you how that pain is running through me and hurting me all over. Truth Be Told, you look at me like I am some invalid who just need to be put out of misery. You know what, you are probably right. Maybe I do need to end this right here and right now. How should I end this though? I am afraid to end my life. I need to fight to survive to help those like me. How can I listen to your negativity and turn it into a positive? I am still young and strong and have a fighting spirit. I can make it. Truth Be Told, you should leave and take your negativity with you. I can see it in your eyes. Even as I speak you become distant. One moment it seems as if you care about me and then the next it is as if you want to jump out the window to escape me and this disease. I sit here in the sun light and ask god what is his plan? Is there more to his plan as my father and my leader? I know he understands me and keeps me here for a reason. I cannot stand your negativity anymore more. I want to be liberated from your evils. Truth Be Told, I can feel it happening now. I can feel myself being set free

from you. You are that thing, that person, and that fear that has held me back.
Truth Be Told.

Life

Life is you
Life is me
Life is every living thing that you cannot see
When you go outside and touch a tree
That is life, helping you to be.
Life is pain
Life isn't fair
Life takes what it is most care
How can it be that I am not there?
But life is and it's everywhere.
Life is chance
Life is sorrow
Life is all the things we dream of tomorrow.
If we knew all that was life
There would be no us.
Life is frustration
Life is mystery
Life is all the crime of the world
It stops on a dime and continues without time
It is the one thing that is worth dying.
Life you
Life is me
Life is everything that you cannot hear.
Just because I can hear you and you can't hear me
Doesn't mean I am dead and you are alive: we are life.
Life fair, but it is even.
It will not take you without a reason.
The reasons are hard
Sometimes unbearable
But life is love
Life is me
We are like family; just because it's LIFE.

Judging You

I am not here to judge you.
I am only here in the capacity to help you.
I am here to instruct you.
To help you find your desired you.
There are several things that you can do.
One; let us begin to judge you.
Why? It's one way I can help you.
When others judge you, you become insecure.
So if you judge yourself; those insecurities go away.
How? Because the words of your enemy,
Will fade off like a distant memory.
You will begin to see the world through new eyes.
My friend you are some step closer to your prize.
Two; let us find out what hurts you?
So we can find something new, what say you?
The third would be to guide you.
On your journey, through your memory, back to a happier you.
In the end, you will see.
What is what that brought you back to thee!

Diversity Is….

Diversity is an Opportunity
To evolve beyond the limitations of our mind and body,
Diversity is Good Business
We use to drive the varieties of economic success in our world,
Diversity is Our Strength
It gives us our own individuality,
The downside of Diversity
The emotional and physical effects no one mentions,
Diversity is a Disease
Controllable and curable if detected early,
Diversity is Natural
A genome we inherited at birth: Our description of sorts,
Diversity is the one true thing we all have in common
We are human after all, cells of individuality,
Diversity is Chaos
Reeking habits on all those who don't understand it, misinterpret, or
plague it,
Our Diversity is our Greatest Strength
Pushing us to different levels of social, emotional, and physical stability
Diversity is Universal

Forgive

Forgive us...
For not believing in you when you needed us,
For believing someone who didn't trust us,
For turning you against us,
For feeling like you betrayed us,
Feeling like you did us wrong....

For taking advantage of you,
Using your kindness against you,
For going away without you,
Believing that we could make it on our own,
To be the ones to take care of what went wrong...

Forgive us...
For lying in your face,
Painting you as a disgrace,
Giving you false hope of friendship,
For allowing you to believe we wanted kinship,
We are vile and in hardship...

For our selfishness,
Our loyalties that we promised endless,
Taking what was yours,
Faking that you had pours...

We are in a world where we ask of little,
But where we do a lot to belittle,
In time what we need,
Is what we have to exceed,
All we need to do is
Forgive.

Forgiving

Forgiving is the essence of man
For it release us from constraints
Frees from the pain within
And creates a better life for us
To enjoy to the end

Cry for Help

Forgot us on the curve
She had a lot of nerve
To come back with a silly excuse
Why should we listen, what's the use?
She says the same things anyway
Only when things don't go her way
I try to forgive her for her ways
But I don't know if I could handle this for several more days
I need you to come for us now
Please tell us you will, when and how
I feel like I am alone
The oldest to protect us, in this dome
Please come for us before it is to late
I know you don't like her, you hate
Please don't leave us here alone,
Or I promise you we will run, be gone.
This is the last letter I can send
I hope it gets to you to before the end
Before our last cry for help!

Dear Friends

Dear Friends
I would like to tell you
Sex has many consequences with every action
You tell me
That it is ok and that it isn't dangerous
You tell me
To just go with it like everybody else goes with it
You tell me
I can't hang if I can't slang
I would like to tell you
It's your funeral, so don't expect me to show up crying
So during our next encounter
You better bring your health to the table
Or else I will just say, "I told you so!"
And your words won't fly
For what you can't deny
I told you to be safe, but you choose to use haste.

I

I was a child when it happened
My life wasn't mine, no use adapting
The streets were never my own
No place to call home
Always someone there trying to take my throne
Through:
Death
Lies
Videotapes
They tried to hit me, take me, like Watergate
All around me did nothing but hate
Because I could articulate
All because of a mother I had
Who taught me right; didn't let me go bad
Like all the other's in the world
Chasing after the girls
No education under their belt
They think they're going somewhere
From:
Drugs
Fast Money
Power
A word they can never tower
It is a shame it had to be this way
But I need you to read and hear what I say
I am on the throne
I am no king; just got the best bone
Cause I got:
Brawn
Brains
Education
To help heal and release our nation
That's all it takes is one
One, who is, I

Roommate

How can I let it stand?
When I don't like this person, the man?
He doesn't know how to stop
When all I went him to do is hop-
Out the door or window-
Leaving me alone in my spot,
My crib
I am not a baby with a bib
Only a college student with a lot to do
A lot on my plate, you know, don't you?
I don't like this kid
He needs to kick rocks; skid.
He tries to get in my business
Why he all up in my business?
It's not his to miss
Or Is this how he gets his bliss?
The manager never told me he was like this.
I should have never trusted him.
He different like the rock-band kiss
The manager I mean
Should've told me the kid was just like him.
Then I never would've missed
A crazy kid like this!

Stop Trying to Suppress Us

They coming in our classes
Trying to paint over the mirrors and glasses
Changing all the literature
Making it what they want; their architecture
They trying to suppress us
Holding our votes and words against us
They don't want to help us
Going on television blaming us; causing a fuss
Got [people] about to cuss
We don't need their words
They need to stop trying to suppress us
We [people] can stand on our own
But we need them to protect us; not leave us alone
They don't want to help:
Black
Latin
Asian
Jew
We are all different, giving something new
In this world, in this continent, called America
They try to suppress us
Turning us against one another
Fighting our own brother
Not the real enemy: the suppressor
It was us who held them up
Giving them what they wanted
They just took it and turned their nose up
Leaving us wanting
Jobs
Life
Better Healthcare
All the like
They are the joke
They play us like a musical note
The suppressors
No one will sequester

Them: hold accountable
For their lies
Deceit
Propaganda
Bigotry
They protect their interest: the rich
Ship our jobs overseas: isn't that a bitch
They bring hate to the table
They tell the world we are unable
To:
Work
Take care of ourselves
Learn
Educate
And validate
But they take away our freedom
Voter suppression
Media demolition
They need to stop suppressing us
Like Michael Jackson said,
"They don't care about us"
I sit here; I regress
My mind has too much to say
The visuals, too much to play
So all I have to say,
No vitriolic intentions
Just words from an American citizen
"Stop trying to suppress us."

Temper

A flame burning within me
I can feel myself beginning to heat
The blood inside me boils
The steam from my ears hitting the walls
My eyes closed in a squint
My lips are now spread thin
My friends tell me to calm down
I shake them off; and then I frown
I have a temper
That I cannot control
They told you to leave out the door
You looked behind you and stayed at the floor
My temper began to flare real badly
I am about to beat you down,
Run or I'll do it gladly
1
2
3
That's the count
You are still standing there.
Oh well, time is out.
4
5
6
7
Once again my temper rose to heaven.
8
9
10
I begin again
You almost got knocked out
But I took the time to count ten.

Angel's Song

The song of the angel's covers the earth,
Finding its way to the body; returning to the dirt.
The hymn of their song brought forth a crowd,
Too remove the mask covering the town.

The town was masked by the death of a boy.
That was killed by a mad man and his toy.
The song of the angels broke the town's ploy.
The town in the worlds view was starting to annoy.

Justice has not been done,
For the young black boy killed with a gun.
The death of the boy brought the nation to its knees,
The parents are still waiting for the cops to answer their pleas.

The angel's mourned for the unjust done,
The man accused is on the run.
Hidden behind the shadow of the mask,
The cops tried to erase and down play his past.

The angel's song called to the world
Too watch over every young boy and young girl.
Parent's sat down with their kids,
And all too simply explained what is.

The song of the angels can still be heard
By the groups that gather to be heard.
Even though justice has been undone,
The angel's song is of the time to come.

They sing of justice for the future,
Also, for the town held together by a suture.
There are things still left unsaid
But the angel's song looks ahead.

But God

All I can say is, "But god!"
Without him my life would be hard.
He led me through rough pastures,
I could not see his goal, but he led to what I was after.
His guidance given to me, his faithful child,
My hand holding his; I followed him and smiled.
"But god!" was there to help me move.
Where? I'm not sure. But he improved my mood.
I called upon him many times this day,
Every week, I made sure a message went his way.
He answered me the following day,
Today, I didn't even have to say,
"I was not feeling well. My spirit was low."
He automatically knew, and gave me his love.
They say, "God is good."
But I say, "But god!"
There are too many words to describe him.
No one is right or wrong; we just praise him.
As long as you believe he is our savior.
He will know you as his child, our father.
Send up a prayer to him when you can.
Because he helped me from my position, I was a tin can.
So all I can say because I was amazed,
"But god" works in many ways.

Our First Date

I stand outside your door
Smiling to myself;
Wonder why I set this date,
The cold weather I deplore.

From the conversation we just had
I know you are not ready, this makes me sad.
But I can imagine what you would wear
How you would dress your hair.

The coldness is getting the best of me
Or is the fact that I cannot wait to see
How you look in the dress I choose for thee
That is my only plea.

I walked up to the door
Knowing you was home, in your room, on the second floor.
Just as I knew she would your mother answered the door.
With a frown on her face; something else I deplore.

I did not know what to think
All I could do was blink.
I had never seen this look before;
I wonder why it was directed at me: standing at your door.

You came and stood beside her
The tears had been running along your cheeks
Those you couldn't hide either
Looks like you had been crying for weeks.

You told me after your mother left
It was time to move on
To forget all we had shared; all we had left
You said you could not love me anymore: I had to move on.

I could not find the words to utter
So I started to slur: a mutter.

How could you say those words to me?
You don't love me anymore. I need to leave and let this be.

I have known you for years
We grew up together and shared the same tears
How could you leave me this way?
When all you could have done was say:

How you truly felt about me
And all I had to do was look in your eyes and see
The truth that you had been keeping from me
Those who only knew: you, your mom and Jeremy.

One last look at you was all I could do
One last look in your eyes: hoping it was just a joke, a surprise.
I can't describe how I feel to you
After all the things we've been through.

I remember when I first kissed you.
We were ten then.
You blushed, I thought you cute even then.
I never knew this would be our last cue.

I lay in my bed staring at the ceiling.
Trying to make since of all my feelings;
Was it love I felt?
Or just lust I was dealt?

I don't know what it was
But I know I am lonely without you,
Without us, what was!
A love I knew to be true.

I lay in this bed
After a long hour cry
From my lips, a sigh
When I remember there was NO
Our First Date!

Every Time I Am Away

Every time I am away,
I think of you in every way.
My feelings for you I want to reveal,
All the ways you have helped me heal.
When I think of you, my body rumbles like a storm,
With you my love, this is becoming the norm.
My love for you makes we weep,
It cover's my feelings that run deep.
I try hard not to focus on you,
But I can't seem to keep you out of view.
Your words always inspire me,
Too think of ways to make you happy.
I can't promise you I will always make you happy,
But I know it won't be intentional, I'm not that sloppy.
Every time I think of you,
I see you smiling in my view.
My body tends to shiver,
Every time I hear your words, your whisper.
I tell you these things with all my love,
I hope you can see it, come to me, my love.
Every time I am away,
I constantly think about you in every way.

To Heal Every Girl, Boy, Woman, or Man

Remove your hands from your eyes
And see the brightness inside
You have made the mistake of being hidden
From the world, yourself, and true feelings within
Your voice has been snatched from you
From your lover, your friend, your beau
Speak to me with your eyes
Write down everything through your cries
I am here to help you
To turn you from old to new
You can trust me
Just listen to my words; lean against me
I am a friend
I will be with you till the end
Let your heart guide your hands on the paper
Tell your story for the world and your neighbor
You have gone through a great deal of trauma
You had your fair share of life's drama
Remove your hands from your eyes
And smoothly glide them across the paper; no more lies.
Tell the story you have kept within
Every little girl, boy, woman or man
Should see and hear your story and say, "Amen"
Pull your story from within
But only if you write the truth
Will your voice heal and change the world
Giving it something new
To twirl
There is nothing that can't be said;
Since you are alive and not dead
It can be said,
From here or on top of the roof
However, you choose,
Your message can reach across the world
Sheltering every human being
To heal every girl, boy, woman, or man

Take a Chance

Sitting under the glistening night sky
I took off my jacket and undid my tie
Placing my jacket on the ground
I sat down before I was found
I opened a book that I choose by chance
And read from a place of circumstance.

From this book I learned to take risks
To get away from all that was bliss
If I choose circumstance
I would not have been able to take a chance
And fight for my life
Using my father's army knife

I had to get away from all that was evil
Because it was turning me into a beagle
From this book I took the chance
In the end I was only enhanced.

I escaped the prison of that bliss
Only by a few inches, a near miss
I found this tree up high on a hill
So my enemies could not make the kill
My mother always told me, life is chance
So I went ahead and took a chance.

Speech to You

Your vulgar routine is predictable.
It lacks merit but it's debatable.
You're too narcissistic,
I can't believe no one ever told you,
How could you miss it?
Every day it shines through.
You note yourself a 'pacifist'
But you really can't see past your fist.
I know it's hard for you to understand
But I've figured you out; nothing to withstand.
You're too much of a superficial being
Do you understand what I mean?
I don't know why you are so shallow,
But it could be a ploy unseen.
But I am too mellow,
To break face and become what is not seen.
You don't like me
I already know, you don't have to say anything.
But if you cross me,
I would be the last you remember watching.
But the future cannot predict our clash
Our honors will one day mash.
I maybe a silent lamb
But I will not let you attack, I be dame.
So sit back and enjoy the view
This is my speech to you.

Poverty

In the most horrific of time
When no one has a dime
This place is just beyond your door
Need I tell you something more?

When you are left in the dark
And you can only hear the sound of a dog bark
You are in that place of horrific time
Where all you will know is crime.

Peeking through your window
You see no one that you know
You must feel as if you don't exist
To be in a time and place like this.

With no money in you possession
With food as your obsession
How can you continue on?
When your place is set to be gone:

You just lost your job and all that you were worth
Now all you can do is starve and watch your children hurt
In the most horrific time
When no one has a dime
Need I say anything more?

I wish I could help you, you see
But I am just like you, I be
I have no money and no possessions to my name
We and they are one in the same.

Our brothers and sisters around the world are just like us, you know
They too have no one to turn to except the people they know
Sometimes those people don't care about them
So we just end up singing a hymn

I can tell you that life will get easier
But I don't think you would want me to lie either

So I will just tell you like I tell the others
Share and don't be a bother-
We are all your brothers

When all we have is one another
It is important to share to help the other
I know it is hard to give what you have
But it is better to share, than to live with half

You and I and they are one now
Just like the people with all the money, wow
We live a lot differently
Than those people in the city

They have forgotten us
They forgot how to trust
They believe we all a criminals
So they left with little minerals

We cannot survive alone
But we can't take each other home
In this most horrific time
When we all are struggling to make a dime

The world sees us as a perish nation
Without all that is given and taken
We live in poverty,
That's worse than all of thee.

But we know how to survive
And we learn to strive
To help us leave this place
The world has spaced
Named "Poverty"

How I Truly Feel

My cool is starting to dissipate
I am trying so hard not to hate
But it is hard I must admit
I just don't know how to quit
I think of all these ways to say,
"I hate you."
You don't know how much these words are true.
You try to impose your stature on me
But even then you can't get over on me
I block you at every turn
You words don't even burn
I sit in my room to keep conflicts at bay
I listen to all the noise outside my door,
Hit my leg and all I can say is hay,
Because you I deplore.
If you only knew what I wanted to do
You would probably try to do it first
Competing with me on cue
But not meeting up with my spirit and fist
I don't even have to touch you though
All I have to do is what you already know
The things you hate that I do
You acting brand new when I do
I can see it in your eyes
Hear it in your voice
You don't like me; that's no lie
But you have to live here; you got a choice
I don't like you
But I don't try to make you into a fool
This is something you are good at
Making everyone around you into a fool
Got people dropping their hats
About to lose their cool
But I haven't yet
I still keep it cool
This is how I truly feel
You already know the deal.

Loss of Freedom

A cold winter's night, I a slave
Sit on my knees, crying at my mother's grave.

I, too young to save her, from master
Gave her my tears; my love for ever after.

She was killed at the hands of her owner
He wanted more and felt this was the way to disown her.

He looked at me with coldness in his eyes
I wanted him dead, wanted him to be my prize.

The wind blows all around me, I cry
My mother is no longer here to teach me, I sigh.

The spirits tell me it is my time to lead
I am no longer scared to bleed.

In my mother land, Africa
We never had to beg, or work for them.

Now we have lost everything, the loss of freedom
We must now take it back, the cost of the kingdom.

In the end, my mother will be revenged
I will still weep in the end.

Not only for losing my mother
But for those who lost their lives and who loved her.

From the beginning was our loss of freedom
Now we have chance to get it back, for our kingdom.

Dream Girl

My every desire wrapped in one,
Tender as mist, loveable undone,
Your skin will be a soft hew of brown,
Your body the shape of a figure eight,
Oh, how I would admire you on our first date.

You will be, with your toned, expressive arms,
A vision of perfection that a sculptor could not imagine,
You are my dream girl, a girl who is as smart as lovely,
With a brain far superior than that of any other,
You would have been chosen for me by your mother.

So, why bother with all the formalities?
When you already know that you are mine, formally,
My dream girl, your aroma calls to me when all others are silent
The purr of this aroma murmurs what you want to say to me;
The call of woman to a man- the man she has chosen.

You are the dream that I see as my reality,
No formalities between us,
Only possibilities that we make when we see each other,
Because you are mine and I am yours, dream girl.

I can see what you see and finish your thoughts before you
Just like you can see what I see and finish my thoughts,
Only my dream girl can do that.
Your eyes would be able to read me deeply,
Even when I am sleepy; I could not lie to you.

My dream girl would have to be flawless,
Not perfect in every way, but confident about her beauty,
She would have to be confident about her body, mind, and her soul.
She would melt in my arms when I held her.
My Dream... It's nothing compared to the real thing, I believe.

Dreamers dream dreams that may not come to light
For those that do come, we are the lucky ones
For those that do not have to work a little harder to see it through,

I have already seen my dream
Today it has come true,
Why?
Because in my arms tonight,
The woman I thought I would never have,
Is my Dream Girl

Dream Girl 2

Eyes as bright as the dawn sky
The winds on the horizon like your morning sigh

I lay here and watch you sleep
The sight of you makes me want to weep

Weep, my fear of losing you, my dear
Living without your voice in my life, I need to hear

I kiss your forehead before I get out of bed
I choose not to wake you but to make you breakfast instead

Dream girl, of all your life, and the world of possibilities
I know how much I love you and all your humilities

I found my star in you
My love seems to grow the more I am around you

Dream girl, for in life we have our challenges
But with me you will experience them with fewer grievances

You walk down the stairs in your morning rob
Walk into my arms and I kiss your ear lob

Good morning, I say to you
You are my shining star come true.

Gay & Lesbian

Why does everyone stress who we are?
When we are just like them, but,
On a different bar:
We can see that we are different,
But we're not that complicated,
So, why treat us like invalids,
When we're really not that different?
You say that we are created under his image
Then you turn around and say, "You're going to hell!"
Because we are not like you,
The person supposedly created from his image,
Who always plays the game of scrimmage?
We get beat because of our difference.
We're told we can't marry because we are the same.
But we must be different in order to live.
For being different, you say, takes away an advantage to give.
We cannot raise children; you say it will influence them negatively.
How can someone be influence negatively?
When we are the same as them:
The people they see who are gay & lesbian.
I cannot sleep because I wonder why,
How can I be different?
This cannot fly.
You are like me to every other guy
And she is like her to every other girl.
In time you will see.
What this thing means to me.
Gay & Lesbian is not a disease,
But just another phase,
Just like a cool breeze.
We are forever more,
Will be known as,
Gay & Lesbian

Goodbye John

You made me cry for the last time
I admit I have tried to get away from you before
Only to be drug back here to this place: not anymore
I have taken the advice of my friends
To leave and to go to a place where you will never find me
I have taken the liberty to change who I am
Never again, will I let you control me
I cannot blame you for all that I went through
It is my entire fault, all on me
For not being strong enough like I was raised to be
For not fighting to get away like my family asked of me
You have taken me from my family
And have taken them from me
I must admit I am alone
But I can't stay here anymore: for I will surely be gone
With this said. I will leave you with a prayer
Please don't look for me. It will cause a great despair
I am no longer yours. I am free
I am free to find what I did not want to see
I will let others know of your existence
Your abusive ways, condescending tone, and impassive resistance
But I can't go through the trauma again
I must learn to heal and move again
I will always love you for who I thought you were
And I forgive you; the person I wish I hadn't knew
In time I hope you will grow: Or at least go back to the person I knew
That will not make me come back to you. But it will make you a better
you.
For now, all I can utter is, Goodbye John.

I Am My Fathers Son

I am my father's son because he is the one who created me.
He is the one who put the vision of peace and equality in me.
He gave me life even before he was sure he wanted to.
He taught me that love was most important to whom I gave it.
He taught me the meaning of being a man.
Showed me all the things that I could accomplish being a good man.
He was there when I needed him the most, comforting my mother and I.
He held me and told me bad dreams where the devils work.
He showed me that all a man had was his life and his worth.
I am my father's son and he is his father's son.
I learned a lot from this man I only knew briefly, for life took him away from me.
I could not believe all the things he taught me would cause him to leave, leaving my mom and me.
I thought it was my fault that he chose to leave.
In the end it was he that wanted to leave.
I am my father's son for all the things that he was to me.
A visionary,
A hero,
A father to me!
He gave my mother and I a life we wouldn't forget
In the end we lost him and the world had split.
I am my father's son because I choose to raise my children like he did me.
Leaving them when it was time for them to grow,
He gave me a new lesson that I will use to let others know-
Life teaches how to grow.
I am my father's son.

My Reason

For all the wrong reasons I gave into you
I knew I shouldn't have but you made me feel new
In the past, your words have never come true
Appearing here or there from out of the clear blue
How could it be I was led to trust you?
When in my heart I knew you were too good to be true
You let me down more than once
My friends told me to leave or to commit a response
I just want you to know that I love you
I told you those words a time or two
I know you could never say them in return
But all-in-all I wished this relationship had never burned
I just want to tell you I am leaving: My reason,
You never though highly of me; it felt like treason
You always found time for everyone else; expect me
I knew in your heart you deplored me
This is a final good bye: My reason
You never loved me
And I didn't want to stay a trophy: gee
For you use and for me to die
I wanted you to know, this is no lie
That is just my reason

Promise

I stand before you, your husband to be
I give to you, my life and a better part of me
With these words I say to you
I promise to make your dreams come true
If I falter on that promise
Remember, it's not because I wasn't honest
From my heart I give you my love
Let it fly with you like a dove
It will take you past my emotions
And carry you with my every motion
There are words that can be called a promise
But I will always remember to keep them honest
Once we are home, you will see what I mean
Don't worry, you will not turn green
I will lay you down on the bed
And lay a kiss on your head
I will undress you slowly
While you giggle, softly
Looking at you bare,
I knew I could just stare
You undressed me to
And then I came to you
In my arms you went
I kissed you till you were spent
Then I whispered in your ear-
As I laid with you on the bed-
"I will love you always," I said
"That I promise."

Mr. BIG

Just because I am round
Doesn't mean you can bounce me around
I may walk swaying side to side
Don't mean you can make fun of my hide
You see me and you point your fingers
Your words wrap me like your throwing ringers
I hid my tears behind my eyes
If only I could turn your words to lies
I am BIG
Not a little skinny TWIG
This is who I am
So keep with your jokes I don't give a dame
You skinny people
Always make fun of the big people
I am working on my weight
So step away, don't hate
The year is 2012
My goal is 175 by 12
You can't tell me you not surprised
All up on, you go nowhere to hide
All us BIG people
Can do just like you TWIG people
So go on and walk away
I need to hit the gym today
I know those words surprise you
We not all eat, but we chew
I will see you at the end
I will be a buck sixty-five plus 10
Remember what you called me: BIG
Tomorrow I will be a little smaller but not a TWIG
So go on back on and relax TWIG
And let me do my thing because I'm Mr. BIG

Piano

Hidden, in the basement of the old apartment;
Dust covered and grown old, the years were cruel
A child sitting at its keys I see, only a faint memory
The keys, black and white, I see him play in agreement
Each key with a settle term of endearment he sings.

In spite him, the mastery of song which he is
Takes him back to a time when he wept, let him be
The memories he tried to hide underneath those keys
Kept them hidden from his dreams
Seeing them at night;
Behind his secure screams.

A person appeared beside him at the piano
He knows this person, his teacher, yes he knows
The person who sits next to the this boy
Memories hit him full force, adjusted his course.

He remembers the reason he has never played the piano after this day
This man, his teacher, betrayed him in such a way
I see his hands move from the keys to the boy
I tried to scream him and plead
No use, he could not hear me, was this a dream?

He touched the boy and stole his self-innocence from him
He did nothing to advance his feelings for him
He got up and left the room
Never to return, never to loom;
In the end, he lost, but at what cost?
His life innocence and love for the piano.

Radio

I used to sit in my room listening to the radio
Tuning in to different channels I did not know
All was the same on one station after the other
I could not tell them apart from one to the other
That all changed when I got to one station
That station I cannot remember, hesitation
Your voice came through the speakers, clearly
I knew I had to meet you, really
I turned up the radio to hear you sing,
You gave my life meaning, with one swing
It was late in the evening when I heard your voice
Amazing, because mine was so hoarse
I could not hold a tune to you,
You let your voice shine through to me
From that day on, I wanted to meet you
For you to be with me
The radio is still on that channel today
Listening and waiting for your song to play
I keep it on this channel, no play
Hoping to meet you one day
I sit by every evening, listening to the radio
Wondering when they would play my song, sitting next to the window
I just sat there listen for your song, you know
Listening to see if it would come on my radio

Revealing

Turning the table onto me: he forget, it was him I knew it would be
The person who my spirit told me it would be; why was he lying on me?
We talked about solutions for this problem nearly every day
Yet, he was the one that held down his head, the one who could not play.
I found out this day, that he was the one to sway
From a monogamous agreement between us, to say
I was the one who changed the agreement anyway.
The table had turned; the line, drawn
It was not me who messed up, but he who drew in the line.
I was told by our superior to stay fast
Never break from my higher class
But it was he who broke the agreement that lead me to be last
Last, to reveal my spirit had been right in the past.
The person who broke the agreement, the truce
Had lied and thus become a recluse.
I have done my deed for which I must live
Now he has to do his time and learn to live and give.

Searching for Her

I'm lying in my bed staring at the ceiling
Dreaming with all of my feeling
Searching for that someone special
To come into my life from the meadow
I don't know where I'll find her
But I hope I don't have to barter
For her love I know it's special
It's wrapped around me like a seashell
It keeps me warm through the night
It makes my life shine so bright
Sex is not the only thing that's on my mind
I couldn't care less if it drove me blind
I'm just looking for that someone special
To come to me form across the meadow
To fill that void in my life
And to be my wife
To bare all my children
To keep them safe until till the end
I know soon I will find her
One day that time will occur
I will have to set the trap
To lure her to my wrap
I will be advancing more
While I'm searching for her

Miracle

A miracle falters
From a reality it alters
Even after the miracle is won
There is only little fun

Minorities in Motion

People of color that never fades
When you see us; you see many shades.

We don't have that many facades
But we have been here many generations: decades.

Lost behind centuries of pain: our memories have fade
Our senses pick up natural aromas as if they were scented glade.

We don't hold to many offices of powers
However, we do build great walls and great towers.

Towers that have stood the test of time since our existence
Towers that have guided us, shielded us, and healed us from hate during
our resistance.

A resistance that cost millions of lives
However, gave us minorities in motion, a chance to thrive.

Yesterday, we live on the ground
Today, we live in house, in town and around.

It seems as though we are making a come up
But we know better: things are not always what they seem, muck up.

We translated the bible for our survival
Went around the Americas; preaching at revival.

Minorities in motion are not just my people
It covers those like us: brown skin or dark people.

They speak a different language: live across the way
We befriended them and helped each other along the way.

We are not targets of a crime
This crime most people care to drop; not wanting to waste a dime.

We continue on our road of struggle
Hoping progress in our world continues and doesn't buckle.

We are "Minorities in Motion" with one destination in mind
To be considered equal with those who think we are less than there dime.

We have survived hundreds of years: shed millions of tears
But we have survived by moving. This is why they call us: "Minorities in Motion."

Adversity
In the face of adversity
You can only hope to find a small snippet of diversity
In the eyes of the bully in front of you
A person who torments you because you are new
Knowledge in you will bring great relief
Conquering adversity is just the side effect of belief
Defeat the bully without hands
In the end, you will make amends
In the face of adversity

Hold Me Now

Hold me now,
Hold me forever,
Promise me, that you will hold me whenever:
When I need you now,
I want you to stay, by my side, always.
Hold me when we're together,
Hold me when we're apart
Hold me forever,
And I'll never let you part.
These words I speak to you so ever gently are words from a lover
This lover you have known you entire life,
One you wouldn't compare to another.
I have seen you cry and I have seen you smile
Hold me now,
Hold me forever.
I was there when you lost your way
The person you turned to, to help you on your way:
I told you a secret, one you never forgot:
Hold me now,
Hold me forever.

Joy

Dear little child
How I long to see you smile
From the day that you were born
I knew that you had been torn
You were not what I expected
But I more than accepted
The gift that gave me 'Joy'

You are more than just my child
You are my heart that beats aloud
God gave us you with a smile
The day your mother had you Child
When they popped you on your bottom
I knew that you would stop'em
With one little peep
You made everyone weep

Our little angel
You taught us how to mingle
With all those like you
Shinning in a purity so true
Your mother and I gave you a name
We thought fit you just the same
The name we gave you
Is perpendicular to,
The reason we named you,
'Joy'

Behind Your Eyes

The mystery I am trying to solve
Your defenses I seek to dissolve
Lies behind your eyes
The portal to your heart
A heart that I am trying to mark
Lies behind your eyes
I am trying to capture that mystery
So we can create a history
Lies behind your eyes
The key to that mystery
You; the mystery
I am blocked by your eyes
Your heart I want to be mines
The mystery I am trying to solve
The defenses I seek to dissolve
Behind Your Eyes

Open Book

Open me up and I am blank
The single cover inside a book-
I am a page- you must write what you think
Pull from your mind your words that will let them take a look.

When you are done, I will have your words
Words that inspired you to write in me
You gave me life with these words.

When you read me to your friends
They will ask, "What inspired this?"
You will say, "It came from within."

You will reveal to them your story
You will not want to be in a hurry
Your story is too important to rush
You will want everyone around to hush

You will give them blank books at the end
Ask them to please write and then begin
In the end, they will return
In their stories all that they have learned

Write This

I write this instead
of saying roses are red
I leave this for you
not mentioning violets are blue
Valentine's Day nears
My heart pounds can't you hear?
I send you my love
that wounds around you thick like a glove

Surprise

I thought you might try to hide
You know what day it is?
Can't you tell by my stride?
Surprise, here it is
The day lover's love
The day our hearts sore like a dove
Can't you tell by my stride...?
How I created this red, white, pink surprise.
It is all just for you
For you this Valentine's
Red, white and pink surprise...
Now close your eyes
I hold in my hand something for you
That will bring tears to your eyes
Now open up and see with your eyes,
Surprise!

Life Lessons

I'm learning to live
And I'm learning to be polite
And I'm learning to get my life out of evils way
Not falter, when I hear the drill
|And I'm learning not to curse|
And I'm learning not to steal
And I'm learning (though it sometimes really hurts me)
|Not to lie|
And I'm learning to help others
|When I can, only when I can|
And I'm learning that it's much
Much easier to be nice

Words with Romance

Words with romance
Are used to enhance
One's feelings for another
Bringing people closer together
Without words of romance
There would be no need to dance
No romantic movies
Or romantic comedies
Or romantic novels
With romantic music remedies
Words with romance
Creates the vibe essence
Without it
The light of the heart isn't lite
Words of chance
To break the ice
Words of romance
Tell to someone nice.

Climax of Heart

My heart reached its climax
The moment I touched you
Your skin, warm and smooth
I took off my hat
And then I kissed you
And nibbled you too
The soft sigh that escaped your lips
Sent my heart past climax to bliss
I pulled you close to me
And bit your anatomy
We connected in such a way
We didn't want to pull away
When we heard the noise outside
Someone was coming, we had to hide
My heart reached its climax
Knowing we would get caught
I didn't care anyway
You were my only thought
To carry away

I Want to Make You

I want to be the person that makes you take a second look
Makes you stop and keep watching as I walk away
Keep you focused on my rear: the view of your day
Making your temperature rise several degrees above normal
Your pulse quickening under your skin: not the heat, just a woman's
sexual inner thermal
I want to make you run after me
Make you so unsure that you touch my arm to get my attention
The fear gone and so the apprehension
Nervous until your eyes takes in all of me
Fully clothed, making your mind visually view all possible scenarios
Thinking of how far all this goes
I want to make you burn under my intense visual contact
Make your back sweet and muscles retract
I want to make you ask me over
Not for a one night stand: but for many nights over
I want to make you scream of pleasure
Before I even enter you: I want to see how you will measure
Up against the other women
Whom I have the pleasure of gripping
After a full meal and a glass of gin
To the bed: One hand in them and under their chin
I want to make you make them all a memory
For the one's I didn't do: To never come to me
I want to make you scream my name
Never to say another man and never to cast blame
I want to make you mine
In both body and spirit
Those are just my words I want to hear you say
After orgasm number five, "I want to make you mine."

~Love~

Love
Is only
Given to those
Who can handle it
Best
Out of all others
Who only use it
For a selfish purpose
And end up losing it
In the end

Leaves Fell

Leaves fell on the autumn morning,
Yesterday, everyone was mourning,
With the falling of the leaves,
Fell a man and the trees.
The leaves that fell were very old,
Just like the man, whom story they told,
They did not just fall and lay on the ground,
Like the old man, they turned brown.

A gust roused the leaves,
That fell from those trees,
Those leaves turned red,
To pay respect to the dead,
They rested on the ground
Next to the body that was bound
For eternal resting
They began their nesting.

Leaves fell from the trees
Late that autumn evening
A gust roused them and carried in the air
They did not stop,
Until they came to a block,
That carried the scent of the man's chair.
They went to the door and knocked,
And the gust let them fall,
No just falling without cause
On a mat is where they were found
They made the person pause.
On the mat of the old man's house:
It said in these final words-
I love you and will miss you, just look where the leaves fell.

Moving

Leaving this place of memories
The place where I began all my dreams
Moving to a place far way
To get out of temptations way
Moving, the last thing I wanted to do
I knew I couldn't be happy without you
I know this is the only way
That I can get you to stay
In my heart, always,
Moving, far away like you wanted
Hoping you will still want me
I will miss you while I am gone
Hoping your heart doesn't turn to stone
I will never forget your face
How you held it high with grace
You never let my faults hold you down
You always showed up when needed in town
The people here respect you most
So I must leave here like a ghost
You don't want to see me now
Oh, how I hope you will change, you just don't know
How far I will go
To be here with you now
So I will not say goodbye
But one day I will return and say hi
You will ask why I moved
And I will saw I didn't want to be rude
You would be much wiser
More wiser and happier
To keep me in your arms
Only, too keep me moving.

Fear

Scale the wall. Fear is tall
Fear is the thing that tries to conquer all
Scale the wall. Fear is opposite benevolence

Fear is the non-giver of chance
Scale the wall. Fear is not hope
Fear is just like dope
Scale the wall.
Fear is tall
Managed by a scary doll

Conquered by benevolence standing by on the wall
Fear has no chance at all
It can only be managed by a doll
Far from you cause you stand tall

Hope lies on the other side
Ready to embrace and support
Life's eternal goodness.

Fathers of Protection

Fathers of Protection
Lead against the war of violence
That plagues our Nation and our Families
Which destroys the cultures and relationships we have built to create a
Sustaining future with many possibilities for our children
And their children whom will undoubtedly
Become the enemy of our enemy we have left them.
Fathers of Protection
Gives love to his family and friends without wanting in return
The love that he is giving out
Instead he wants to insure that his family is safe
Even when he is on the front line to defend them
Against a terror so horrific it frightens him to be in its presence
But as the Father of Protection he is allowed such feelings
That could possible get him harmed and dead
We the children look up to our fathers because of the magnetism they
present to us
And the skills they leave us to help ourselves and our families
The reason we considered them Fathers of Protection is because that's
what they are
The Protectors who are fathers
Our mothers are the nurturers who nurture us when they are gone
And provide for us when we are alone and who love us when we are
afraid
They are our mothers
But our fathers are our protector
They love us just the same but have different ways in showing it
They protect us, they are
Fathers of Protection
Leaders can describe many of them
But father describes all of them
They are here for us and we are here for them
They are forever
Fathers of Protection

THE END

Of

If I Told You

My Inspiring Poems

Written by:

James Jackson III

Made in the USA
Charleston, SC
19 September 2014